TEEN LIFE

I HAVE BEEN CYBERBULLIED.

NOW WHAT?

CAITIE MCANENEY

ROSEN
PUBLISHING®

New York

For Kathy Mahaney,
whose life inspired so many small acts of kindness

Published in 2016 by The Rosen Publishing Group, Inc.
29 East 21st Street, New York, NY 10010

Library of Congress Cataloging-in-Publication Data

McAneney, Caitie.
I have been cyberbullied. Now what?/Caitie McAneney.—
First edition.
     pages cm.—(Teen life 411)
Includes bibliographical references and index.
ISBN 978-1-4994-6138-1 (library bound)
1. Cyberbullying—Juvenile literature. 2. Bullying—Juvenile
literature. 3. Internet and teenagers—Juvenile literature. I.
Title.
HV6773.15.C92M34 2016
302.34'302854678—dc23
                                                    2014039602

Manufactured in the United States of America

CONTENTS

Y|ou turn on your computer and hold your breath. Signing on means facing rude remarks, hurtful comments, or rumors about you. There seems to be no way to escape the negativity. If you've faced a situation like this, you've been cyberbullied.

Cyberbullying is threatening, harassing, or embarrassing someone through technology. Cyberbullies might use their phones to text threats. They might use e-mail to forward hurtful messages or private messages that were shared with them. They might use instant messaging or social networking to spread lies or post cruel remarks.

While one rude comment can certainly hurt someone, cyberbullying usually happens over a long period of time. As the cyberbullying continues, victims may face depression and anxiety. They may feel isolated as cyberbullying pollutes their online social life. Some victims feel there is no way to escape their tormentors because the Internet is practically everywhere and cell phones are carried all the time.

Unfortunately, the more technology bullies have access to, the more ways they can get to their victims. Justin W. Patchin and Sameer Hinduja, directors of the Cyberbullying Research Center, summarize their recent findings on the center's website. They report that nearly one-fourth of youths admit that

Some teens skip school to avoid in-person bullying, but avoiding cyberbullying is much harder. It causes unwanted stress in a seemingly safe environment.

cyberbullying has happened to them at some point in their lives. They also found that 16 percent of youths admitted to cyberbullying others.

In their 2009 study, Patchin and Hinduja also found that cyberbullying and traditional bullying are closely related. If someone is a bully at school, he or she is more likely to be a bully online. Similarly, if someone is a victim at school, he or she is more likely to be a victim online. The Internet is merely a tool for wider tormenting. It often encourages bad behavior and gives bullies the power to invade the private lives of their victims.

According to the National Center for Educational Statistics in their 2011 study, nearly 30 percent of students say they're bullied at school, and much of that translates into cyberbullying as well. What makes cyberbullying different from traditional bullying? Both involve a person, or multiple people, harming another person, physically or mentally. Both may involve spreading lies or rumors. One big difference, however, is that traditional bullying is often left at school. Cyberbullying follows its victims home. A traditional bully can physically hurt the victim or spread lies around school, but a cyberbully can spread lies all over the world. While home is normally a place to get away from the torment, a victim of cyberbullying may feel there is no safe place. The Internet is everywhere, and sensitive information—such as lies, threats, rumors, and private pictures and conversations—spreads quickly.

Although many cyberbullies justify their behavior by saying their actions were funny or not a big deal, the truth is cyberbullying has serious effects on victims. This resource will explore why cyberbullying happens, different forms of cyberbullying, and its consequences. It will also discuss how to prevent cyberbullying and get help once it's happened to you or someone you know. When you're the subject of hurtful texts or posts online, it may seem like your privacy is gone. But there are ways to recover from being cyberbullied. There is hope for regaining your online identity, your reputation, your safety, and most of all, your sense of self.

THE MANY FACES OF CYBERBULLYING

Each instance of cyberbullying is unique; no two cyberbullies, victims, or circumstances are exactly the same. Cyberbullying cases range from annoyance to harassment. Some cases happen once while others happen continuously for months or even years. Some forms of cyberbullying can be forgotten, while others will live forever on the Internet.

While all cases are different, there are a few main types of cyberbullying. Learning the different ways a cyberbully can reach you is the best tool to keep yourself safe and identify cyberbullying when it happens.

As you read about different forms of cyberbullying, ask yourself: Has this happened to me? Have I done this to someone else? Have I witnessed bullying like this? What kinds of consequences does it have for those involved?

SENDING HURTFUL REMARKS

Sending hurtful remarks is a common cyberbullying tactic. Patchin and Hinduja at the Cyberbullying Research Center found mean or hurtful comments were one of the most common forms of cyberbullying. In their 2010 survey, they found that more than 14

Why did they choose me? That's a question that runs through the minds of many victims. Bullies often gravitate toward people who are different, passive, or easily upset. Victims may be different in terms of appearance, race, gender, sexual preference, or disability. Passive people make good targets because they seem too scared, shy, or weak to fight back. Cyberbullies may think it's easy to get away with picking on a passive person. According to Marcia Eckerd in her article for Smart Kids with Learning Disabilities, passive victims make up about 85 percent of all bullying victims.

Some victims are provocative, which means they're quick to get upset and impulsive in the things they do, say, or post online. These people are often targets because the bullies can "get a rise" out of them. These victims might cry or ineffectively try to fight back, either physically or verbally. They might engage the cyberbully in an online rant, which adds more fuel to the bully's fire. This provocative behavior is sometimes associated with ADHD (attention-deficit/hyperactivity disorder). Acting out against a bully often continues the cycle of violence, which is further continued if the provocative victim decides to become a bully to feel better.

COMMON VICTIMS OF CYBERBULLYING

percent of their survey population had endured mean or hurtful comments online in the past thirty days.

The aim of hurtful remarks could be revenge, jealousy, or attention. Many times the comments are used to build the cyberbully up—to make him or her feel better—while breaking the victim down. With a few keystrokes, cyberbullies can successfully get through to their victim, leaving the victim feeling powerless.

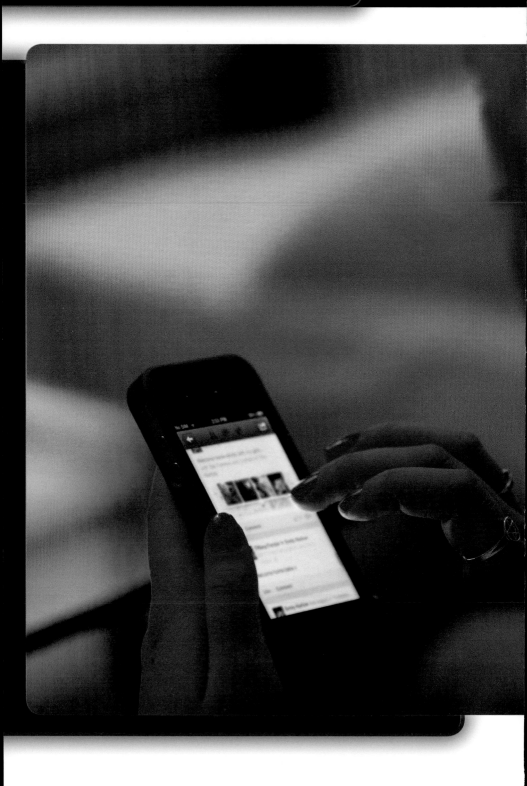

The Pew Research Center (2013) reports that 78 percent of teens have cell phones, and of that number half have smartphones. Teens can send and receive hurtful remarks via texting and social networking any time.

Hurtful remarks are commonly seen on social networks. Facebook and Instagram are two websites that allow users to post photographs, which make them common places for this kind of cyberbullying. Facebook and Twitter are websites that allow users to update statuses and post to another person's profile, which are additional tools for cyberbullies. The cyberbully can either create a hurtful post or comment on something a victim posts.

Hurtful remarks come in many different forms. A common target for cyberbullying comments is a person's appearance. Cyberbullies might comment on a person's height or weight. The cyberbully might call attention to someone's acne or the fact that he or she wears glasses or braces.

Cyberbullies often make hurtful remarks about people they see as weak or inferior in some way. That makes people with disabilities or special needs easy targets for cyberbullies. According to Marcia Eckerd in her article for Smart Kids with Learning Disabilities, people with learning and social disabilities, such as attention deficit disorder (ADD) and autism, are especially at risk for being cyberbullied. Even if a victim doesn't have a disability, a cyberbully may label the victim with words that suggest he or she is disabled in some way.

A person's lifestyle choices include how that person dresses and acts and whom he or she decides to befriend or date. Cyberbullies often target people with lifestyle choices that are different from theirs. Lesbian, gay, bisexual, and transgender (LGBT) individuals are another frequent target of cyberbullyies. In fact, according to a 2013 study by the Gay, Lesbian & Straight Education Network (GLSEN), the number of LGBT youths who have been cyberbullied is nearly three times more than non-LGBT youths who have been. About one in four LGBT youths admit to being cyberbullied specifically because of gender identity or sexual orientation.

Whether a victim is gay or straight, a cyberbully might call attention to how many relationships a person has had, whether many or few. They may harass someone because of an alleged sexual act. They might also call someone out for acting against gender roles. Negative

Social media often brings personal relationships into the public view, which can lead to cyberbullying. Even otherwise happy couples like this one may face criticism and hurtful comments about their relationship.

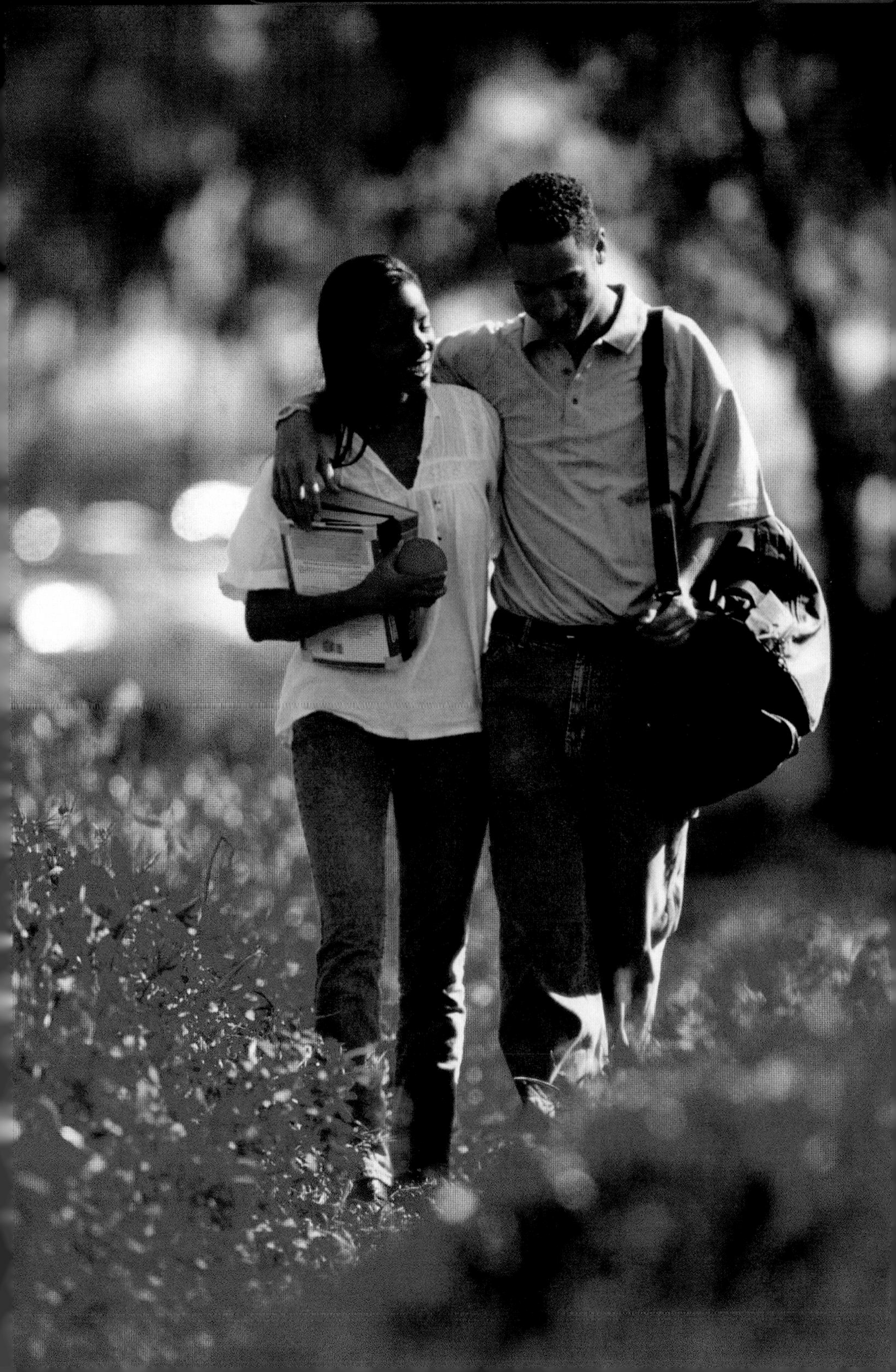

remarks about a person's lifestyle choices are especially cruel because they attack who the victim chooses to be.

Hurtful remarks break down a victim's self-esteem and make the Internet an unsafe environment. It can be hard to accept yourself when it seems others are against you.

Spreading Lies and Rumors

Have you ever played the game Telephone? One person whispers a sentence to another person and it goes through a line of people. By the time the sentence is said out loud at the end of the game, it's usually much different from the one that started it. That's the danger with spreading lies and rumors. They might start out small but they can end up bigger than the bully ever imagined.

According to a 2010 study performed by the Cyberbullying Research Center, more than 13 percent of youths admit to being the victim of rumors online. Of course, there were lies and rumors before the Internet. Even now, this happens at school and in other public places. However, the Internet is a different kind of place. It includes networks of people we know and those we don't know and reaches all over the world.

There are many kinds of lies and rumors a person might spread. They might make up something about a victim's sexual preference or dating history. They might

Cliques are groups of people who don't easily let others join them. Cliques have power in numbers and may spread hurtful remarks or gossip against someone. The isolated victim may feel helpless.

WHY DO PEOPLE CYBERBULLY?

What makes a bully? According to the American Psychological Association, bullies tend to have negative attitudes and beliefs about others. But bullies often feel negatively about themselves, too. Bullies often come from family environments that have conflict. They tend to think negatively about school and have academic trouble. Both bullies and victims lack social problem-solving skills, meaning that they don't know how to interact with others or deal with natural conflict in a healthy way.

George Steffgen and his colleagues found in their 2011 study that people who cyberbully may have less empathy for others. A lack of empathy might make people more likely to cyberbully because they can't feel the pain they're inflicting on another person.

Bullying online makes it easier for people to join in on the harassment, promoting a group mentality. If many people are involved, a person might think it's okay to join in because they can't get in trouble. No one will blame them directly because they didn't start it, and "everyone's doing it."

Perhaps one of the biggest reasons people who wouldn't normally bully others in real life can cyberbully is because it all happens behind a screen. Saying something behind the screen takes a bit of the guilt or shame away because you can't see how it affects the other person. Some people find the Internet to be a great disguise. They can hide their identity by either creating a new one or posting anonymously. The human connection is gone.

MYTH

If you go online often, you're more likely to be bullied.

FACT

In an article published in *Psychology Today*, Michele Ybarra—president of the Center for Innovative Public Health—says only around one in seven youths are cyberbullied when they log on to the Internet. Other factors make cyberbullying more likely, such as a person's personality, their interpersonal skills, and if they're bullied in person.

MYTH

Cyberbullying happens only on social networking sites.

FACT

In Larry Magid's article for the *Huffington Post,* Ybarra says nearly 10 percent of youths have been bullied by phone and 14 percent have been bullied by text message.

MYTH

Cyberbullying has replaced traditional bullying.

FACT

Ybarra says in-person bullying still happens almost twice as much as cyberbullying. Those who are bullied offline are more likely to be bullied online.

MYTHS AND FACTS

spread a rumor about a girl being pregnant. Rumors, whether they're founded in half-truths or purely on lies, are extremely damaging to the victim. They shape the way people treat the victim and interpret the victim's words and actions.

A cyberbully who starts a lie is like a kid pushing a snowball. It gains weight and power as it rolls through more people. Rumors can pass from student to student and even on to teachers, employers, and family members. While hurtful remarks are often direct attacks on the victim, spreading rumors is a cyberbully's way of getting others involved. This can keep the victim from being treated fairly or from being considered for a job or a scholarship. It can isolate the victim, making others turn away from him or her.

A cyberbully can spread more than just words. To make people believe their lies, some cyberbullies circulate pictures to support their lies or embarrass the victim. Picture-editing programs, such as Photoshop, make it easy for a cyberbully to manipulate an image to incriminate or embarrass a victim—even if he or she has done nothing wrong. The cyberbully can broadcast these forged pictures or videos with the rumors as false evidence.

How does a cyberbully spread rumors and lies? Social networks make it almost too easy. Cyberbullies might post status updates or pictures that set up the rumor, allowing all their friends to see them. Some people have hundreds, or even thousands, of Facebook friends,

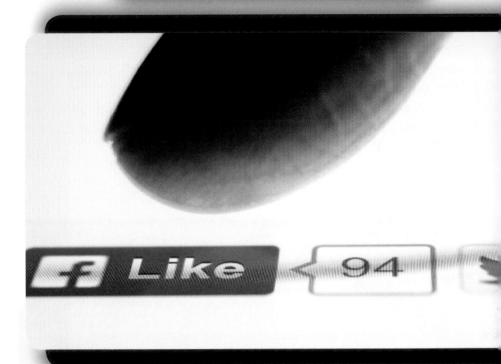

Have you ever seen a hurtful or rumor-spreading Facebook post? The small action of clicking "like" could involve you in the hurtful cycle of cyberbullying.

so the rumor can spread quickly. They might tag the victim—or link to his or her account—in the status. They might even post right on the victim's wall.

One cyberbully is enough, but many times it doesn't stop there. Other people may support the cyberbully by liking or forwarding the status, video, or picture. They may share the rumor with all of their friends, who then share it again. In the worst-case scenario, the rumor or lie could be spread to thousands, or even millions, of people.

Nev Shulman, center, fell in love and eventually found out that the woman he'd been talking to online made up the identity. The movie *Catfish* is a documentary of his experience.

CREATING FALSE IDENTITIES

How do cyberbullies get away with cyberbullying? Tracking someone down or finding his or her true identity can be difficult online. That's because some people have online identities that are separate from their true identities. They create profiles with fake names and pictures to fool people into thinking they're someone else. Some cyberbullies even hack, or break into, their victims' accounts and pretend to be them. They might use a victim's account to post things so everyone believes it was the victim, and not the bully, who did it. In a survey, Patchin and Hinduja found that almost 7 percent of youths admitted that someone had pretended to be them online in the thirty days preceding the survey.

False identities are a powerful and destructive tool for cyberbullies. They can hide behind made-up personalities to harass someone without getting in trouble. But even worse, they can use false identities to trick people into trusting them. The victim may get emotionally attached to this person. In popular culture, this is informally

called catfishing. Some people "catfish" others to trick them and expose information that's given in secret. Other people want to get someone to like them.

The growing trend of catfishing inspired the MTV series *Catfish: The TV Show*, in which people contact the show's host, Nev Shulman, when they or their loved ones believe they're being catfished. As a fellow victim of catfishing, Shulman listens to people who are being catfished and goes on a mission to find the truth. Often the truth is hard to find and even harder to hear.

Megan Meier, a thirteen-year-old girl from Dardenne Prairie, Missouri, was a tragic victim of catfishing. She suffered from depression, insecurity, and attention deficit disorder. But none of her issues seemed to matter after an attractive boy named Josh Evans sought her out via Myspace. Megan developed a deep emotional attachment to Josh online. One day, Josh started sending her hurtful messages and sharing things that she'd shared with him. Other people responded with spiteful messages, too. Upset and confused by Josh's betrayal, Megan killed herself on October 16, 2006.

Weeks later, Megan's parents found out that Josh Evans had never existed. His identity had been created by the family of a girl Megan was no longer friends with. They made a false identity to trick Megan. Megan's parents say she died believing Josh was a real person. Megan Meier's tragic suicide put cyberbullying into the national spotlight and showed everyone how dangerous false identities and hurtful remarks could really be.

CHAPTER 2

Social networks and text messaging make it easy to communicate with friends. It's simple to send information about what time and where you will meet up. You can send pictures and videos back and forth for fun. But sometimes private information, pictures, and videos are made public. In the wrong hands, this media and information can be used against you.

HOW DO CYBERBULLIES GET PRIVATE INFORMATION?

There are many ways a cyberbully can tap into someone's personal life. Some cyber-bullies, including siblings and other relatives, may live in the same house. Others may have been friends at one time until a falling out. Other cyberbullies are masters at hacking computers. The best way to keep your information and media from being stolen is to learn how cyber-bullies can gain access to your private world.

Giving Information

Whom do you trust? You may trust your family, boyfriend or girlfriend, or closest friends. You may think these people would never do any-thing to hurt you. You may think giving them information might be harmless. Think again.

According to the National Campaign to Prevent Teen Pregnancy, nearly 70 percent of teens who sext send the pictures to someone they trust. A broken trust may make you feel hurt or scared.

Many people have had their private information or photographs leaked to the public after they've broken ties with someone they used to trust. This can be a best friend or a boyfriend or girlfriend. That person may have been the most caring person when you were friends or dating. However, after you cut ties, that person can take information—sexual pictures, private conversations, secrets— and share it online.

You may even feel compelled to give information, pictures, and videos to someone you haven't even met. The Internet makes it easy to connect with and open up to people you don't know. You may meet someone in a gaming community or social media website and establish a connection after only a short time. You might trust a person so much that you agree to give him or her private information or send that person pictures and videos that you wouldn't want made public.

The problem with interacting online is that you never know with whom you're actually talking. People who use false identities to take information are often able to manipulate their victims into trusting them. They're often very smart, too. They'll think of evidence they can use to prove they're the person they're pretending to be, such as pictures or accounts from other people. Although you may see a picture of an attractive person your age, the person might be older and more dangerous. This person might try to gain your trust so he or she can ask you for personal information, such as your full name, school, address, phone number, or Social Security number. He or she might ask for explicit pictures or videos of you posing naked or in an incriminating position. Sometimes, these people aren't just cyberbullies—they're sexual predators.

To be safe, never give information to anyone you haven't met before in person, and never send private pictures over the Internet. Even if you do know the person, you want to be careful. A cyberbully or predator could have hacked the account of someone you know to get the information from you. If you're wondering if someone you're talking to online is actually the person you think he or she is, ask about it in person or over the telephone.

Stolen Information

Although some cyberbullies use information that's given to them, other cyberbullies steal information from online accounts. This may happen if you leave your laptop unattended in a public place. For example, if you're using your laptop in the school lunchroom and get up to get a napkin, a bully can either steal your laptop altogether or sign into your accounts and find information.

Someone can also steal information if you use a computer in a public place, such as the library. If you get up to talk to a teacher, a bully can get into your account and look for private pictures or messages. You may also be at risk of having your accounts hacked if you forget to log out of accounts on public computers. A bully might get into your account after you leave the computer. To be safe, never leave a computer unattended and always log out of your accounts.

It's possible for people to hack your computer without even touching it. These people, called hackers, know how to use technology against people. They may be computer experts who want to profit from someone's personal information. Celebrities are at high risk for their information being hacked because hackers can sell pictures and incriminating information for money or share it for attention. For example, in 2012, a man hacked into the personal accounts of celebrities including actresses Mila Kunis and Scarlett Johansson. He stole private, sexual pictures of them to broadcast on

It may seem safe to walk away from a computer in a classroom or library. But even friends sometimes hack computers and post embarrassing Facebook or Twitter statuses as jokes.

the Internet. This is a crime—the man was sentenced to ten years in prison.

Other hackers want credit card or bank information so they can steal money or an identity. To keep safe, never share credit card information—even if it's your family credit card—with anyone you don't know or with a company that doesn't seem reliable. There are many times you may need to enter credit card information, such as when buying an app or shopping online, but make sure those websites seem real and reputable. Download only apps, games, or software that have good reputations. Many hackers break into computers by spreading computer viruses and tracking cookies through downloaded programs.

When Pictures Give Power

When your information is stolen, you might feel exposed, unsafe, and vulnerable. But perhaps nothing can make you feel more vulnerable than having photographs of you spread around the Internet. Pictures can be used as visual evidence against you—suggesting that you're not attractive, you're clumsy, or you did something shameful. Pictures aren't the only weapons cyberbullies have today. Most phones can also take videos, which can be even more incriminating as they expose what you do and say.

In the age of the Internet, anyone is able to snap a picture or record a video at any time. Most cell phones have cameras and smartphones are connected to the Internet, making pictures and videos easily sharable via text, e-mail, or social networks. Cyberbullies can easily use pictures to destroy your self-esteem and give themselves power. Some cyberbullies may even use pictures as blackmail. Although some pictures or videos are just embarrassing, others can ruin your reputation.

Embarrassing Pictures

We've all done something clumsy. Maybe you've tripped in the hallway at school or blurted out the wrong answer in class. Maybe something embarrassing has happened in a public place, such as dropping your lunch or ripping your pants. These embarrassing experiences can make your self-esteem plummet, but usually they blow over in a short time. But what if someone took a video of

If a picture says a thousand words, a video surely says more. It did in the case of Tyler Clementi, a freshman at Rutgers University. He was gay, but not out in public. Few people knew about his new relationship with another young man. However, that all changed when his roommate, Dharun Ravi, found out about it. Ravi used a webcam to take a video of Clementi kissing the man he was dating. Then, he posted about it on Twitter. He and his friend tried to catch Clementi again and continued to tweet about it.

Clementi read Ravi's tweets and knew what was happening. Just two days after the initial webcam and tweet—September 22, 2010—Clementi went to the George Washington Bridge and jumped off, killing himself. His death brought attention to the struggles of LGBT youth and put the spotlight on cyberbullying. Clementi died because of his embarrassment over the very personal video that was passed around for the amusement of others.

THE VIDEO THAT KILLED

you doing something embarrassing? What if someone snapped a picture when you fell in the hallway? The effects of that embarrassing moment can live on longer and can be spread to more people.

Because many students have cell phones, it's common for them to take pictures during the day. But that means no one is safe from having his or her picture taken, and no moment can be completely private. Private conversations or interactions can be spread around the school and around the Internet in no time at all.

Being bullied in person is hard enough, but this girl is also being filmed as her classmates embarrass her. This film could end up online and make this hurtful moment live on.

Some cyberbullies think it's funny to post pictures taken of people when they're unaware. Because they don't know they're being photographed, the picture could make them look unattractive. Or, they could be doing something they wouldn't want others to see. Some cyberbullies post pictures of people with the aim of making them feel bad, thinking it will amuse other people. There are entire websites dedicated to posting pictures of people and rating their attractiveness, usually allowing people to write terrible and hurtful comments.

Party Pictures

If the thought of everyday embarrassing pictures scares you, imagine photographs

Some party pictures send harmful messages. According to a Columbia University survey, 75 percent of teens say that seeing pictures of people partying on social media encourages that behavior in others.

that are taken when you're letting loose. Party pictures can be embarrassing, plus they could get you in major trouble.

Parties are places to be especially careful, as you never know who's watching you from across the room or taking pictures and videos nearby. And with many people nearby, there are lots of opportunities to do or say something embarrassing or make bad decisions. You might see your crush across the room and go talk to him or her. You might get into an argument with someone. You might decide to drink alcohol or experiment with drugs. Drinking and doing drugs will impair your judgment, which could result in poorer decision making.

If you're drinking, doing drugs, or participating in any

other illegal activity, such as vandalism, pictures and videos can be the evidence that gets you in trouble. These images and videos might be shared online or used as blackmail. They could have serious consequences depending on the nature of your partying activities, including being grounded by your parents, suspended from school, or punished by the law.

Being under the influence of drugs or alcohol might make you a target for bullies who think the way you're acting or speaking is funny. This can quickly spiral out of control. In 2012, a high school party in Steubenville, Ohio, witnessed an act of terrible violence. A girl, who is not named because she was a victim, passed out because she'd had too much to drink. She was sexually assaulted at the party, with many of her peers looking on and documenting what was happening on social media. They spread pictures of her, naked and assaulted, over the Internet. Those at the party texted and uploaded pictures to social media, posting videos on YouTube. The boys who assaulted the girl were convicted of rape in juvenile court.

There are steps you can take to make sure party pictures are never taken of you. The first solution is to not go to any party unless your parents have given you permission to attend. Make sure your parents know where you are and who you're hanging out with. If you do go to a party, don't participate in underage drinking, drugs, or vandalism. Remember that people might be recording what you're doing or saying. Act in a way that won't make you feel embarrassed in school on Monday morning. Above all, make sure to always be safe and on your guard, even if you're surrounded by people.

Sexual Pictures

Sexual pictures are perhaps some of the worst kinds of pictures that can make it on to the Internet. These pictures might show a person either partially naked, completely naked, or in a sexually suggestive position. These pictures can be used to ruin someone's reputation, hurt his or her feelings, or even put him or her in unsafe relationships with sexual predators.

Many social networking websites, such as Facebook, have rules against such pictures, but that doesn't stop people from posting them. Once cyberbullies obtain sexual pictures of their victims, they can easily post them to a number of sites and may not be stopped until the pictures are already spread to a wide audience.

How do cyberbullies obtain sexual pictures? Many come from people whom the victim originally trusted, especially a significant other. Sending sexual pictures by text message is called sexting. There are many dangers associated with sexting, and there are many laws against it.

One young woman, Carrie, knows this situation all too clearly. She started dating her boyfriend when she was fifteen, and he manipulated her into sexting throughout their relationship. She says, "He used to tell me how beautiful I was and how much he loved my body and wanted to see it constantly. And sending a picture doesn't take much time, and how could I upset him

According to DoSomething.org, 40 percent of teenage girls sext as a joke, 12 percent feel pressured, and 34 percent do it to feel sexy. Girls report more pressure to sext than boys.

by saying no?" Years later, Carrie found the courage to leave him. She was just starting her career, making a fresh start after this manipulative relationship. But after she broke ties with him, he posted one of the pictures on a popular social forum. He impersonated her so it looked like she posted the picture. Carrie found out about the picture through him, once they'd started talking again. "In fact, he said it so calmly and with a little bit of a laugh, that he had no idea how it might make me feel…as if I deserved it. As if I had done something so wrong to him." Carrie asked him to take it down, but he never did. She didn't have the money to pay to have it taken down or to hire a lawyer to fight it.

After finding out about the pictures going public, Carrie felt her world turn upside down. "I later found the courage to look at the page more closely, and saw that over 18,000 people had viewed the picture and included comments. A picture, taken in the comfort and privacy of my own bedroom, was being viewed by people I could walk by in the daytime and have no idea they had seen it." She added, "How many people had seen me naked? I've struggled with body image issues, and the thought that others—complete strangers—had seen and commented on my completely naked picture was utterly horrifying."

Carrie's story proves that even though you may trust a person, that person may not hesitate to share a sexual picture if you break up. The picture may be sent to peers through text messaging, e-mail, or social networking. It may be sent to parents, teachers, or employers. It may even be posted to websites for the wider Internet community. There are many websites devoted to "revenge porn," or sexual pictures that were taken for a significant other and then posted online after a breakup. These pictures can be viewed by youths and adults alike. Some cyberbullies may post pictures of their victims to get them unwanted and unsafe attention from sexual predators.

Carrie hopes others will learn from her story. She says, "I would advise young people to avoid sexting or sending explicit pictures to anyone, significant other or not. I know that I sent them because I felt like it was all I had to offer to make him happy. How could I say no? Well, my advice is to say no. If they truly respect you, they will be OK with it."

CHAPTER 3

If you've ever been a victim of cyberbullying, you may be all too familiar with its consequences. Cyberbullying affects the way victims think about who they are and what they've done. It affects how people feel about their identities and the people around them. It affects relationships and social situations both in school and at home.

This chapter covers just a few of the psychological and social consequences that cyberbullying has on its victims. It also includes information from licensed clinical mental health counselor Nicole Newcomb, who specializes in treating anxiety, depression, trauma, eating disorders, and substance abuse in adolescents and young adults. Learning about the consequences of cyberbullying can help identify them if they are happening to you, arming you with the tools and coping skills to recover.

A RUINED REPUTATION

The most visible consequence of cyberbullying may be its effect on a victim's social standing. A person's reputation consists of the thoughts, beliefs, and feelings that other people have about that person. On the one hand, a person with a positive reputation might be seen as

This girl is being isolated from her peers. A negative reputation caused by cyberbullying can isolate a person, possibly making him or her more likely to act negatively in the future.

funny, friendly, confident, and popular. On the other hand, a person with a negative reputation might be seen as weak, strange, ugly, and unpopular. Cyberbullying can quickly take people's reputations from positive to negative. Their social circles can shrink until they feel isolated from those around them.

Mental health counselor Nicole Newcomb says, "Cyberbullying changes social standing depending on how severe the bullying, how many people are partaking in supporting the bully, and how the victim handles it." This means that the worse the bullying—the meaner the harassment, the more people involved, the more often it happens—the more a person's reputation might suffer.

If one person bullies a victim, the bully may be able to keep friends on his or her side. The more people on a person's side, the more support the bully might feel he or she has. As in traditional bullying, having a support system can help a victim feel protected from harm. However, the more people who are involved—a whole class, a whole school, a wide-ranging Facebook group— the more a person's social standing may suffer.

A person's social standing also depends on how he or she feels about the situation. Newcomb says, "More times than not, the victim will perceive their standing as being lowered simply because they're embarrassed and anticipate a change in social status." Acting embarrassed, aggressive, or overly defensive can reinforce a negative reputation. It can make the victim isolate himself or herself before others can do it. If a victim handles the situation with positivity and grace, his or her reputation might stay about the same. However, if the victim handles the situation by overreacting or responding aggressively, his or her reputation might suffer even more.

Self-Esteem

A person's self-esteem is confidence in his or her own abilities and worth. Self-esteem can be affected by a person's thoughts about his or her intelligence, physical attractiveness, and social standing. Other people's thoughts and comments about a person can also affect his or her self-esteem.

According to Elizabeth Venzin, founder of Australia's organization Mind Shift—the National Self Esteem Initiative, low self-esteem may put someone at a higher risk for developing depression.

Patchin and Hinduja found in their 2010 study for the *Journal of School Health* that there's a significant relationship between low self-esteem and experiences with cyberbullying. And the more severe the remarks—from annoying to threatening—the more of an impact they can have on a person's self-esteem. Newcomb notes the difference between traditional bullying and cyberbullying and why cyberbullying can be worse for one's self-esteem. "The ability to cyberbully has increased the frequency and intensity of the verbal and emotional abuse. As a result, one's self-esteem is exposed to attacks more often and requires a higher level of confidence to defend itself. Typically, [an] individual's self-esteem is not prepared for this level of harassment."

People's self-esteem is often related to how they feel about their appearance or their body image. One person might feel too short, while another might feel overweight. When body image breaks from reality, a person can develop an eating disorder, such as anorexia or bulimia.

People with anorexia may limit the food they eat to very unhealthy standards, or they may eat a lot and then make up for it by not eating, vomiting, or exercising too much. People with anorexia reach less than 85 percent of what's considered normal for their height and age. Newcomb adds, "They begin to genuinely believe they are fat despite being significantly malnourished. They truly believe they are ugly." Bulimia is another dangerous eating disorder. People with bulimia are often normal weight or just under normal weight, but they go to extremes to control what they eat. People with bulimia often binge, or eat a lot, and then purge, or vomit. This can cause severe health problems.

Cyberbullying can affect a person's body image and, in some cases, could lead to eating disorders. Newcomb says, "Something as little as hearing a peer talk about their clothing size and calories can lead a teenager to feel inadequate and start assessing their weight. The pressure compounds once bullying is introduced." If a cyberbully posts unflattering pictures of a person or comments about his or her weight or looks, the person's body image can go from positive to negative. And if the person's body image is already negative, the situation can get worse. However, Newcomb stresses that often many things need to fall into place for an eating disorder to manifest, such as family history of eating disorders, tendency to strive toward perfection, anxiety, and other trauma.

ANXIETY AND DEPRESSION

Cyberbullying can also lead to anxiety and depression. Everyone feels anxious or sad once in a while, but some people suffer from mental health disorders that interfere with everyday life.

Anxiety is an excessive reaction to stress. It might feel like fear, nerves, or panic. Anxiety makes some people avoid certain situations, people, or objects. Social anxiety is stress that comes from being around certain people in certain situations. Cyberbullying can heighten a person's social anxiety, leading him or her to actively avoid those situations or feel extreme stress in public places, such as school. Victims of cyberbullying may feel self-conscious. Low self-esteem can make them feel worthless, embarrassed, or awkward.

Newcomb comments, "Teens already think that people are always looking at them and judging. Cyberbullying confirms these beliefs and consequently increases anxiety that creates a preoccupation with one's inadequacies." Imagine walking down your school

It may seem awkward to talk to adults about cyberbullying or the resulting depression or anxiety. But positive support can help you deal with the situation in the best way possible.

hallway after seeing a bully post something about you online. You might feel as if people are staring and whispering about you—whether they are or not. "If someone is already struggling with social anxiety then it becomes exacerbated," Newcomb adds.

Major depression is extreme sadness that lasts for a long period of time. People who suffer from depression may find it hard to enjoy activities they used to enjoy and may even find it hard to sleep, eat, concentrate, or communicate with others.

In 2010, Jing Wang and his colleagues at the National Institutes of Health published their findings in the *Journal of Adolescent Health*, stating that victims of cyberbullying experienced significantly greater levels of depression than bullies or people who are both bullies and victims. Newcomb agrees; she says, "Bullying can lead to social withdrawal, isolation, and depression."

As with anxiety and eating disorders, depression happens because of a number of factors, including family history with depression, lack of support, and trauma. However, cyberbullying can take someone with preexisting depression and make it even worse. Newcomb says, "If consistent, [cyberbullying] can lead to long-lasting emotional problems. If an individual is already experiencing other risk factors for depression, then cyberbullying can definitely be the straw that breaks the camel's back."

If you're a victim of cyberbullying who suddenly feels sad for prolonged periods of time and unable to live the way you used to, you may have depression. If you suddenly feel nervous or fearful of social situations in a way that interferes with learning or relating to others, you may have anxiety. Tell a parent, doctor, or other trusted adult if you feel this way. These mental health issues can be helped with the right resources and support.

SELF-HARM AND SUICIDE

Extreme cases of depression and anxiety sometimes lead to devastating consequences, such as self-harm and suicide. Whether this will result depends on the frequency and severity of the bullying, the number or influence of the bullies, and how the victim deals with the situation.

Another form of self-harm is substance abuse. Substance abuse is repeatedly using drugs, such as alcohol, pain pills, marijuana, and narcotics. People who use these substances often becomes dependent on them over time. They may feel they need that drug to feel normal.

According to the National Center on Addiction and Substance Abuse at Columbia University, American teenagers who spend time on social networking sites are more likely to smoke, drink, and use drugs. They also found that teens who have been cyberbullied are more than twice as likely to use tobacco, alcohol, and marijuana than teens who are not cyberbullied.

Why do some victims turn to drugs? One reason is that drugs sometimes offer the kind of mental escape that victims are looking for. It's a way—a dangerous way—of temporarily trying to escape the real world. Some victims might do drugs to try to fit in with a social group or make themselves look cool. Others might do it as a cry for help.

In some severe cases, substance abuse can lead to overdose, which can be deadly.

SUBSTANCE ABUSE

Although some people can shrug off hurtful comments, others are tormented by them. Newcomb comments, "Bullying does not directly lead to self-harm. However, it does have a significant impact if other risk factors are present or if self-harming has occurred previously."

There are many ways that people can harm themselves if they're feeling emotional distress. They may starve themselves or isolate themselves from others. They may take a more active route and bang their heads against things or burn themselves. Some people cut themselves with sharp objects.

What are some coping skills you can use if you ever feel depressed? If music is calming, listen to your favorite songs. Others may relax by going outdoors for exercise.

Cutting, like other forms of self-harm, is a way that some young people cope with their overwhelming feelings. It often brings a sense of control and relief, putting physical pain in the place of mental pain. Many young people hide their self-harm from others by hurting themselves in ways and in places that no one else can see. That makes it hard to get accurate statistics about self-harm. However, the American Foundation for Suicide Prevention noted that in 2012, 483,596 people visited a hospital due to self-harming behavior. They estimate that nearly twelve people self-harm for every one person who commits suicide. Some young people get their ideas of self-harm from websites that promote it, which can be dangerous and life threatening. These websites, like cyberbullying, are just another way that young people can suffer at the hands of irresponsible online content.

What if someone cyberbullies themselves? A new trend is cyber self-harm, which unlike physical injury, happens online. People might post mean or hurtful comments about themselves, either in private or in a public forum or social network. Why would people post negative things about themselves? It might be a way to give self-hatred an audience or a cry for help with anxiety or depression. It may be a way to get attention from peers or to have negative commentary noticed and replaced with compliments and support.

Cyber self-harm likely had something to do with the death of Hannah Smith, a teenager who committed suicide after receiving multiple messages telling her that she should kill herself. When she committed suicide, an investigation into the source of these tormenting e-mails found that 98 percent of them were sent from her own computer.

According to the Centers for Disease Control and Prevention, suicide is a leading cause of death among teenagers and young adults. Nearly 4,600 young lives are lost each year in America to suicide.

In 2010, Patchin and Hinduja researched the correlations between bullying experiences and thoughts of suicide. They found that young people who experienced cyberbullying—either as the bully or victim—had more suicidal thoughts and were more likely to attempt suicide than those who weren't involved. They also found that victims were more likely to have suicidal thoughts than the bullies.

Why would someone resort to taking his or her own life? The answer is complicated. Newcomb says, "Suicide is not an overnight decision and like eating disorders, has many precipitating factors. By the time that a suicide has occurred, there have already been many unsuccessful attempts at coping by the individual." We all have ways of coping with emotional distress, such as reaching out to a friend or family member, listening to favorite music, or writing in a journal. However, some people who suffer from depression and anxiety may find that none of their coping skills are working to make them feel better, which can make them feel hopeless. "At the point of committing the suicide, the victim genuinely feels there is no other way out of their suffering," Newcomb adds.

Unfortunately, there have been many suicides linked to cyberbullying, as in the cases of Megan Meier, Hannah Smith, and Tyler Clementi. Although it's never clear if cyberbullying was the true reason for their suicides, these severe cases show how cyberbullying can traumatize a person until he or she feels there is no other way out. That person may feel that the ridicule will never stop, that the lies and rumors about him or her will continue to spread, and that there's nowhere that's safe anymore. If you or anyone you know is having thoughts about suicide, contact the National Suicide Prevention Hotline at 1-800-273-TALK [8255].

KNOW YOUR RIGHTS AND LAWS

If you've been the victim of cyberbullying, you may feel helpless in defending yourself. It's important to know that there are laws that can work to keep you safe and get you the justice you deserve.

While there are no federal laws that deal directly with bullying, there are some cases that are covered by harassment, sexting, and discrimination laws. Each state has its own laws when it comes to issues related to cyberbullying. What laws don't cover, your community and school's rules and regulations might cover. Research your state and local laws and school regulations before taking action.

Do you think you're experiencing unlawful harassment from another person? Being aware of your rights may help you realize that what's happening isn't a normal part of high school—it might be illegal.

Cyberbullying Laws

Some cyberbullies may get away with their actions. Today, there are few laws that directly deal with cyberbullying. However, with Internet use on the rise and many high-profile cyberbullying cases in the spotlight, maybe one day there will be adequate laws and just punishment for cyberbullies.

You can tell if you have a case against a cyberbully if his or her actions toward you become harassment, especially harassment based on discrimination. Discrimination means treating someone a certain way because of his or her race, sex, gender, disability, sexual orientation, or religion. Because many cyberbullies torment those who are different from them, many cases may fall under discriminatory harassment. According to Stopbullying.gov, discriminatory harassment is illegal under federal law, so federally funded schools are required by law to take care of a bullying situation based on discrimination.

Most states have laws against cyberstalking and cyberharassment, which are included under their traditional stalking and harassment umbrellas. Because of the increase in cyberbullying, many states are now creating laws that are just for cyberbullying.

Cyberharassment laws usually apply to cases where bullies regularly torment a specific person to cause that person mental suffering. This may cover cases in which the bully sends threatening and harassing messages and repeated damaging remarks.

Cyberbullying, especially cyberstalking, may cause more than just annoyance—it can cause fear. If you're afraid of someone who is harassing you online, tell a parent or a trusted adult.

Cyberstalking is extremely dangerous because it demonstrates a bully or predator's intent to harm another person. In these cases, a person uses the Internet to stalk or harass someone, which shows a serious threat to a victim's safety. A victim may try blocking or avoiding the cyberstalker, but the cyberstalker may find and bother him or her again. In many cases, cyberstalkers can be charged with misdemeanors or felonies. Two teens were charged with felony aggravated stalking in the case of Rebecca Sedwick, a twelve-year-old who jumped to her

The Dangers of Sexting

If you're a minor with explicit photographs—which include sexual acts or naked pictures—on your phone, it's usually considered a crime. Sending explicit photographs is also a crime, as is sending or forwarding photographs of other people. If an explicit photograph of someone is making the rounds in texts around school, make sure you never send it, and notify an adult right away. It's also illegal to promote a picture, even of yourself. If you solicit a picture or ask or bother someone until he or she gives one to you, that's another crime. In the worst-case scenario, a teenager can be registered as a sex offender, which follows that person for his or her entire life.

death after repeated cyberbullying at the hands of her classmates.

Some cyberbullying cases are covered by laws that states have against sexting and child pornography. Child pornography is any picture or video that's taken of a minor, or a young person under the age of eighteen. Some states have sexting laws and some don't. The ones that don't may default to child pornography, so punishment in those places may be more severe.

RULES AND REGULATIONS

Even if federal or state laws don't cover the type of cyberbullying that's happening to you, your school may have rules and regulations in place to stop the cyberbullying and punish those involved. You have

A school is supposed to be a community. Everyone has a responsibility to treat others well. Cyberbullying at school can take the environment from healthy to harmful.

the right to an education. You have the right to learn, play, and participate in school activities in a way that's fair and safe. When cyberbullying interferes with these rights, it's important to report the bullying to your school.

Jeff Rosen *(left)* discusses Audrie's Law, which increases punishments for teens who force sex acts on defenseless people. Three classmates posted pictures of their sexual assault of the unconscious Audrie Pott. She was subsequently harassed and killed herself.

By law, schools have the responsibility to address bullying behavior, especially if it's severe, happening repeatedly, or tormenting a student so badly that he or she can't learn. Schools also have to address bullying when it makes the school a violent, unsafe, or unhealthy place for a person to learn or participate in activities. Cyberbullying must also be addressed if it's based on discrimination of race, color, national origin, sex, disability, or religion.

Although all schools need to address bullying of these kinds, each school may have its own bullying and cyberbullying policies. Check your school's guidebook or website to find out what its rules and regulations are. Some schools may have special rules about the misuse of social networking for teasing and making rude remarks. Other schools may have regulations that limit the use of in-school Internet.

Each school has its own way of dealing with bullies, both traditional and cyberbullies. But in general, all schools are expected to look into a cyberbullying complaint and question those involved without bias. They usually interview students involved, obtain written statements, and communicate with the students about ending the bullying. The school should also follow up with the affected students, especially the victim, to see if the cyberbullying is continuing or has stopped. The school should try to prevent future cyberbullying cases by bringing awareness of bullying policy to the school community.

It's important to educate yourself and others about the rules and regulations of your school and also the rules of any after-school youth programs that you might participate in, including dance studios or martial arts schools. Cyberbullying can happen anyway, and you can protect your rights by knowing what they are.

If you've been bullied in any of the ways discussed in previous chapters, you may feel helpless, alone, and hopeless. It's hard to know how to recover. Making the right moves after any trauma, such as cyberbullying, is the best way to gain justice, keep yourself safe from future attacks, and recover mentally and emotionally. Its important to reach out to the right people who can help, as well as help yourself by taking steps to rebuild your life.

TELL SOMEONE

If a cyberbully has attacked you once or twice online, with no threat of future harm, it may be possible to forget about it, collect yourself, and move on calmly. If the bullying is persistent and starts to interfere with your life online or at school, however, it's important to tell someone.

The people we turn to in a crisis are called our support system. A person's support system can consist of friends and family members. These are the people you trust, those who will be there for you when you're upset, and who will try to make things better.

Perhaps the first people you should tell are your parents or guardians. If the cyberbullying is harsh enough, they may try to contact your school or legal authorities to seek justice for

you or at least to stop future cyberbullying from happening. If you're very upset, they may find you a school counselor or other licensed therapist to talk to, which will help you work through your negative feelings. Your parents or guardians may be the best people to go to first because they will most likely care about what's happening and want to make it better.

Some young people are afraid that if they tell their parents about cyberbullying, their parents will take away their Internet privileges. If much of your social life exists online, this may seem worse than the cyberbullying itself. If pictures or posts you're not proud of are circulating on the Internet, you may be afraid your parents will be upset with you. This happens in many cases of young people who have sexual or party photographs sent around. However, it's important to know that in most cases your parents have your best interests in mind.

If cyberbullying is happening between you and another classmate, or if you witness it happening, you should tell a teacher or school counselor. It's those people's responsibility to make the school a safe and healthy place to learn. Your teacher, school counselor, or principal might investigate the cyberbullying, talk to everyone involved to get the full story, and then deal with the situation the way they see fit. Many victims are

If you experience bullying that isn't too severe or frequent, try talking to a friend. Friends may not be able to solve the problem, but they can listen and support you.

Telling a parent about cyberbullying might be embarrassing. First, identify your feelings. Say, "Dad, I need to tell you something, but I'm nervous and embarrassed." Be direct, respectful, and honest.

afraid to come forward because they may feel that doing so would be embarrassing and bring attention to the situation. However, if the cyberbullying keeps happening and becomes damaging, it may be necessary.

If you don't feel comfortable talking to a parent or teacher, you can always talk to a therapist. Anything you say to a therapist is confidential, unless it involves the threat of serious harm to you or another person. As a mental health therapist, Nicole Newcomb recommends therapy to deal with cyberbullying. She says, "An experienced therapist can guide an individual through processing their thoughts, feelings, and past experiences so the victim can make sense of it, learn how to cope in a healthy way, and work towards bettering their future interactions with peers." A cyberbullying victim can learn different coping skills for dealing with negative feelings and can learn how to act and think in difficult situations. A therapist can also help a victim rebuild his or her self-esteem and deal with depression and anxiety.

Whom you reach out to depends on your comfort level and the severity of the bullying. If the cyberbullying is more annoying than damaging, talking to a friend may be enough. If the cyberbullying becomes threatening, hurtful, persistent, or illegal, though, it's best to reach out to a trusted adult, whether it's a parent, guardian, teacher, school counselor, or private therapist. No matter what, find someone to stand in your corner as you work through this.

HEALING AND MOVING ON

When we experience negative feelings, it may seem as if they're permanent. You may think you'll never recover. But there are ways to cope with the trauma caused by cyberbullying. And in time, you will be able to move on.

Therapists have a variety of coping skills and tools to use when you're feeling depressed or anxious. First, you can engage in positive self-talk. That means thinking positive things about yourself. With cyberbullying, the negativity sometimes seems overwhelming, causing your self-esteem to plummet. The way to counter those negative thoughts is with positive thoughts about yourself. What are your strengths? What are you good at?

A therapist can help you identify positive characteristics you have. Positive self-talk may raise your self-esteem.

What do you like about yourself? Congratulate yourself when you do something good. Think something such as this: I'm proud of myself for getting a B on that tough math exam. I tried hard and I'm a smart person. Or try thinking something such as, I'm a really creative person, and I have the ability to make beautiful art. These positive things can help fight against the negative comments from others.

Radical acceptance is another coping skill. Radical acceptance means accepting yourself, others, and the

situation around you. It means looking at a situation and observing it, without getting caught up in it or passing judgment. You don't have to agree with what's going on, but you can still accept it. Instead of thinking, "That embarrassing photo is public and I can't stand it," you may think, "There's a photo of me out in the public. I accept that and I'm moving past it." Radical acceptance is a difficult skill to master, but it can help in many situations in life.

It's important to also accept what you're feeling. If you're feeling depressed and isolated, accept that you're feeling that way, and that it's OK. Feeling sad over losing friends or being bullied is a normal reaction. Be patient with yourself as you work through these feelings. Telling yourself that it's not normal to be so upset will only drive you deeper into depression. Similarly, if you feel anxious, accept that anxiety. Remind yourself that it's normal to feel nervous in school if you're being cyberbullied. It's normal to fear that people might not like you. Accept these feelings, be patient with them as they run their course, and work toward more positive feelings in the future.

As mentioned earlier in this resource, reaching out to a support system is a great tool for healing. It can make you feel that you're not alone in this. Surrounding yourself with good friends and family will help you realize that there are people who like you for who you are. You

Therapy may take some time to work. But in time, you may gain the skills to overcome your anxiety and depression and unlock the happiness that's inside you.

It may make you feel better to get outside with family or friends. In the woods or at the lake, you'll start to feel far away from the Internet's drama.

might just want to talk to them and have them listen to you. They might understand how you feel and try to make you feel better.

Finally, you can make the choice to move past the situation. You may do this by ending any communication with the cyberbullies. Or maybe you will let go of the anger and hurt that you feel and focus on a more positive future.

LIFE OUTSIDE

When cyberbullying is happening to you, it may feel as if there's no escape. But all you need to do is step away from the Internet. Unplug from your phone and laptop and spend time with your friends in the real world. While you may have many friends on social networks and gaming communities, you can build and grow friendships in the real world that mean more.

How can you nurture your friendships outside of the Internet? Instead of texting or Facebooking your friends, make plans to hang out with them after school or on the weekends. Face-to-face time with

HOW TO REBUILD YOUR REPUTATION

As you move on from cyberbullying, you may feel the need to rebuild your reputation. How can you create a positive image of yourself?

The first thing to remember is that many times, if you don't engage with a bully or act aggressively toward him or her, the situation will eventually fizzle out. It may take a few weeks or months, but many times, the talk of the day becomes forgotten over time.

Having a good attitude and engaging in positive interactions with people will also help rebuild your reputation. Try your best to think and act rationally in the face of cyberbullying and show people that you can handle negativity without turning into a negative person.

To rebuild your reputation online, you can delete any old accounts associated with cyberbullying and create new accounts with advanced privacy settings. Let your online identity be one of positivity and friendliness, and resist the urge to overshare or to engage in drama online. Over time, you may be able to build a reputation for being a person that people trust and want to stand up for.

your friends may help you forget about the cyberbullying you face online and can show you that there's more to the world than hurtful comments and rumors. If you feel that you don't have many friends whom you've met in person, make an effort to meet new people.

You can meet new people by joining a club, activity, or volunteer project. If you like reading and writing, join the school's newspaper staff or work on the literary

1. How can I disengage from social networking while keeping my social life?

2. How can I work on becoming independent from the Internet? What is Internet addiction?

3. Are there any support groups for victims of cyberbullying?

4. What skills can I use to cope with my social anxiety?

5. What skills can I use to focus on school and work when I'm upset?

6. What are some healthy ways to confront a bully?

7. What skills can I use to deal with my depression? Is my sadness normal or a more serious depression?

8. What are the differences between healthy and unhealthy conversations and comments online?

9. I sometimes feel like self-harming. What can I do to cope with my feelings in a healthier way?

10. What can I do to develop my self-esteem when faced with hurtful comments?

Listening to or playing music is a great way to burn off stress and express yourself. Getting involved in an activity like playing in a band can raise self-confidence.

magazine. If you love music, look into your school's musical groups including chorus, band, and orchestra. Whether you love sports, art, or anything in between, there's a club for it! These activities can do more than just help you gain a great circle of real-world friends. They can help you find your passion for something you're good at. If you like art, spending a few hours a day painting can help you forget about cyber-drama and focus on creating something. If you like music, learning how to play the piano can help you focus on express-ing yourself through music. Newcomb agrees, "Go out and enjoy the tangible world and activate your mind, body, and soul! I would advise making a life for yourself outside of the environment in which you were bullied."

What if you see your cyberbullies in real life? Although some may go away once you're disconnected from the Internet, others may be sitting next to you in class or see you in the hallway. First, try to avoid them. Walk a different way in the hallway or sit away from them in class. If they come after you, try not to engage with them. Don't let what they say bother you. And if it does, try not to show it. If they keep it up, report it.

Building a greater life outside of the Internet can help you see what's important—real friends, laughter, and fun—instead of the number of likes or negative comments you get on a picture or post. Newcomb suggests, "If you wish to return to a life online after you have built yourself back up, be cautious and have your guard up!" Remember that if it gets to be too much online, you can always unplug and rejoin the real world.

The best way to deal with cyberbullying is to prevent it from happening in the first place. While there's no way to guarantee that cyberbullying will never happen to you, there are some steps you can take to keep yourself, and your reputation, safe.

There are also actions you can take to stop cyberbullying when you see it. While it may seem as if the cyberbully has all the power, you also have the power to shut down cyberbullying and make the Internet a more pleasant place to be.

KEEP IT PRIVATE

The number one way to keep safe from cyber-bullies is to keep your information and media private. You may choose to not make a social media account on Facebook or Twitter in the first place. Or, if you like to be social online, learn the boundaries between public and private information. Try using only your first and middle name on social media accounts or use a nickname. Some social media accounts make it possible to block others from finding you, so you have control over who can see that you even have an account.

ttings

acebook   Search

Choose your privacy settings

🖼 **Connecting on Facebook**

Control basic information your friends will use to fir

🔒 **Sharing on Facebook**

Use the privacy settings for Facebook to make your profile completely private (only your friends can see it). Unfriend anyone who harasses you and everyone else who supports their behavior.

Never give anyone you don't already know and trust in person your address or phone number. If you meet someone online—especially in a chat room, dating website, social network, or online gaming community—keep as much information to yourself as possible. Try not to give your full name, school name, or any other information someone could use to find you. Never give your Social Security number because this can lead to identity theft. Never give any financial information such as credit card or bank account information for yourself or your family. If anyone asks for personal information, regard his or her actions with suspicion. If a person keeps asking, block or report that person.

You can block people from contacting you on almost all social networks, including Twitter and Facebook. This cuts off access to you so they can no longer contact you or see what you post. You can also block people over e-mail and through your cell phone. Check into your account settings to add blocks.

You can also protect your privacy online by checking the privacy settings of your social media accounts. You can choose what you want the public to view and what you want your friends to view. On some websites, such as Facebook, you can keep information private for certain friends, while allowing others to view your whole page. Check your privacy settings regularly to make sure they haven't changed.

Above all, never post anything online or text anything that you wouldn't want everyone to see. This may sound unfair. What if you have a picture you just want to send to your boyfriend or girlfriend? What if you want to tell someone a secret via text? Though it's unfair, there are ways others can get your information. It can be sent from the person who received your picture or secret. It can be hacked by computer hackers. Or, someone could steal your phone and see all the pictures and texts you've sent. Always be on your guard about what you send. If you want to protect

against revenge porn, don't send sexual pictures of yourself. Besides being illegal, once they're created and sent, they can never be taken back. Don't use violent, discriminatory, or biased language online unless you want that image of you to live on forever. Don't post anything in anger, desperation, or to get revenge because it can be used against you and may hurt others or provoke them to bully you. Keep your language online kind and considerate. Keep your photographs appropriate. Ask yourself: Would I want my teacher to read this post? Would I want my parents to see this picture?

Break the Cycle

There are many roles you can play when it comes to cyberbullying, and many steps you can take to shut cyberbullying down. Bullies have the most power to end it because they can make the active choice to recognize the pain they have caused others, to apologize, and to stop bullying in the future.

An accomplice is someone who gives support and attention to a cyberbully. Accomplices may forward or "like" a post or picture, may help spread lies and rumors, and may start sending rude comments themselves. If you recognize that you're an

> If you think you've bullied someone, reach out to him or her. Apologize for your actions and recognize that what you did was wrong.

A friend tells you that a classmate's embarrassing actions are posted online. It's tempting to watch. However, it's important to show that you don't stand for gossiping or bullying.

accomplice to a cyberbully, remove your support from the bully. Refuse to harass a person just because other people are doing it. Cyberbullies gain many accomplices because the Internet allows so many people to spread and comment on hurtful posts. You may receive a text with a picture of someone and be told to pass it on. In that moment, you have to choose: Do you want to be an accomplice or break the cycle of bullying? If you don't send the picture or post on, then it won't reach as many people, and it may stop with you.

Bystanders are people who witness bullying but do nothing about it. This happens often online because many young people believe that writing hurtful

LABELING PEOPLE

It's not always helpful to label people as bullies or victims. In this book, using those terms was convenient for conveying a general situation, but in real life, a person is more than just a bully. He or she may be going through a hard time right now. The bully may have mental health issues. There may be troubles at home. Bullying others may be a stage that person is going through. Instead, consider saying "a person who bullies" or a "person who has been bullied."

Labeling people makes it seem like the situation is very clear when it could be complicated. The bully could be a victim of someone else's bullying, while the victim may bully others in a different situation. A person may be sending hurtful comments or posts because he or she wants revenge for something that the other person did to hurt him or her.

Labeling also gives the impression that people can't change, that the victim will always be a victim, or the bully will always bully others. In reality, many people change as they mature. Some people's actions are a reflection of the environment they're in. While there is no excuse for bullying another person, changing our language about bullying can help encourage empathy for others and break the cycle of hate.

posts about someone else is normal. A person might be afraid that by doing something, he or she might become the next target. However, by being a bystander, you're allowing the cyberbullying to keep happening.

The best role to play in a cyberbullying situation is the defender. Next time you see someone cyberbullying another person, you can report the bullying anonymously. Many schools accept anonymous tips about bullying. You can also report the mean or hurtful posts to the social media website. The cyberbully never needs to know who turned him or her in. You can even try reasoning with the cyberbully.

If talking to the cyberbully or reporting him or her doesn't work, try to reach out to the victim. The victim may feel isolated and alone. He or she may have low self-esteem and feel that no one cares. By reaching out and letting that person know you're on his or her side, you can make someone feel better and stronger.

If you're the victim, don't be afraid to seek help. There is nothing to be ashamed of, even if a cyberbully is humiliating you with pictures and secrets. Recognize that you have the power to break the cycle, too. You can block cyberbullies, change privacy settings, or delete accounts altogether. If that doesn't work, and if cyberbullying turns into traditional bullying at school, tell someone about it so you can get help.

Spread Awareness and Kindness

You have the power to make your school and online community into a safer, more respectful place to be. You can do this by being a role model of kindness through your words and actions. The way you act may inspire others to act with kindness too.

These students are spreading kindness around their school through a ValenKINDs campaign, which includes service projects, kindness ideas and activities, and posters.

You can also raise awareness about cyberbullying. Post information online about how it happens, how often it happens, and how people can deal with it. Ask teachers if you can make posters, pamphlets, or newsletters about cyberbullying to educate schoolmates. Also, talk to teachers and school administrators about how cyberbullying affects your school. Ask them to help you put together a school assembly about dealing with bullying and treating others with respect.

Getting the word out starts conversations between people so victims might be able to open up about their experiences and bullies can learn from them. A school that

It's not easy to stand up to bullies. It's not easy to defend victims. But even something as small as smiling at someone who is frequently picked on can make all the difference.

communicates fosters under-standing among all students. The antidote to bullying is empathy and kindness.

Think about starting a cam-paign for kindness around your school. Make posters or hand-outs that remind people to be kind, considerate, and respectful. Spread the word about antibully-ing campaigns such as "I Choose." (whatdoyouchoose.org) and the BRAVE campaign through the United Federation of Teachers. Educate people on kindness campaigns, such as Random Acts of Kindness (randomactsofkindness.org), the Campaign for Kindness (campaignforkindness.org), and Rachel's Challenge (rachelschallenge.org). The idea behind many of these campaigns is that one act of kindness can create a chain of kindness that stretches across your school, your community, and your world.

Cyberbullying may seem like a necessary evil of the Internet. It may seem impossible to stop. But remember: there are ways to keep cyberbullying from taking over your life and your Internet experience. There are ways to recover from the crushing blow that cyberbullying may have had on your self-esteem, mental health, and reputation. And there are ways to keep cyberbullying from happening before it even starts. Fight negativity with positivity. Fight hurtful remarks with your own confidence. And most of all, reach out to those who really matter in your life, and leave the cyberbullies behind.

GLOSSARY

aggressive Ready or likely to attack or confront.

blackmail To demand money or services from a person in return for not revealing compromising information about that person.

confidential Entrusted with private information; intended to be kept secret.

default To automatically go back to a preselected option.

empathy Understanding an dbeing sensitive to another person's feelings.

exacerbate To make a situation worse.

explicit Very clear and to the point; not at all vague.

forge To imitate something to trick someone.

harass To repeatedly annoy, bother, or attack someone.

identity theft Illegally acquiring and using a person's private and identifying information, usually to steal money.

impersonate To pretend to be someone else.

inadequate Not enough or not good enough.

incriminate To make someone appear guilty of a crime or wrongdoing.

isolate To cause a person to be alone or apart from others.

manipulate To control or influence someone unfairly.

self-esteem Confidence in one's own worth and abilities.

stalk To follow, watch, and bother someone constantly in a way that seems threatening or dangerous.

tangible Able to be touched or felt.

tormentor One who causes extreme mental or physical pain to another.

transgender Of or relating to a person who identifies with a gender identity that differs from the person's sex at birth; for example, a person is born male but identifies as female.

trauma A very unpleasant or difficult experience that causes someone emotional or mental problems for a prolonged period of time.

vulnerable Capable of being physically, mentally, or emotionally wounded.

FOR MORE INFORMATION

Cyberbullying Research Center
Justin W. Patchin
Department of Political Science
University of Wisconsin-Eau Claire
105 Garfield Avenue
Eau Claire, WI 54702

Sameer Hinduja
School of Criminology and Criminal Justice
Florida Atlantic University
5353 Parkside Drive
Jupiter, FL 33458-2906
Website: http://cyberbullying.us

Justin W. Patchin and Sameer Hinduja run the Cyberbullying Research Center, an online collection of the latest information about the nature, causes, and consequences of cyberbullying. This website provides resources for parents, educators, counselors, and others who work with youth.

Cybersmile Foundation
530 Lytton Avenue, 2nd Floor
Palo Alto, CA 94301
(650) 617-3474
Website: http://www.cybersmile.org

The Cybersmile Foundation is a nonprofit organization that fights cyberbullying through education and the promotion of positivity online. It provides professional help and support to victims and spreads the message of hope and positivity to all.

DoSomething.org

19 West 21st Street, 8th Floor

New York, NY 10010

(212) 254-2390

Website: https://www.dosomething.org

DoSomething.org is an organization dedicated to helping young people create social change. It offers a platform for 2.8 million members to promote their campaigns and gain involvement in a variety of causes, from poverty to bullying.

End to Cyber Bullying (ETCB)

147 West 35th Street, Suite 1404

New York, NY 10001

(772) 202-ETCB (3822)

Website: http://www.endcyberbullying.org

End to Cyber Bullying (ETCB) is a nonprofit organization that works to raise awareness of cyberbullying. It offers information and services to fight cyberbullying and get students, parents, and educators involved in ending cyberbullying.

Internet Keep Safe Coalition

4301 North Fairfax Drive, Suite 190

Arlington, VA 22203

(703) 717-9066

Website: http://www.ikeepsafe.org

The Internet Keep Safe Coalition, known as iKeepSafe, is a non-profit international alliance of policy leaders, technology experts, public health experts, and educators. iKeepSafe keeps up with trends and issues in new technology and how they're affecting children, as well as providing resources for teaching youth about how to use digital technology in safe and healthy ways.

Megan Meier Foundation
515 Jefferson Street, Suite A
St. Charles, MO 63301
(636) 757-3501
Website: http://www.meganmeierfoundation.org
Founded by Tina Meier, mother of cyberbullying victim Megan Meier, this foundation aims to educate children, parents, and educators about bullying and cyberbullying and the way they affect the daily lives of children and teens. In memory of Megan, who committed suicide after being cyberbullied, the foundation also aims to promote change and create a safer and kinder world.

PACER Center, Inc.
8161 Normandale Boulevard
Bloomington, MN 55437
(888) 248-0822
Website: http://www.pacer.org/bullying
PACER's National Bullying Prevention Center is a leader in social change to stop bullying. It spreads awareness about bullying as a serious community issue and provides resources for students, parents, and educators.

STOMP Out Bullying
220 East 57th Street
9th Floor, Suite G

New York, NY 10022-2920
(877) 602-8559
Website: http://www.stompoutbullying.org

STOMP Out Bullying is a national antibullying and cyberbullying organization that focuses on preventing cyberbullying, in-person bullying, and digital abuse. It educates people against hatred, violence, racism, and homophobia, and teaches solutions on how to respond to bullying.

Tyler Clementi Foundation
P.O. Box 54
Ridgewood, NJ 07451-0054
(201) 670-1818
Website: http://www.tylerclementi.org

Founded by the parents of Tyler Clementi, a victim of suicide due to cyberbullying, this foundation is focused on promoting acceptance and respect for LGBT youth. They speak out against bullying, cyberbullying, and hostile environments that negatively impact LGBT youth.

WEBSITES

Because of the changing nature of Internet links, Rosen Publishing has developed an online list of websites related to the subject of this book. This site is updated regularly. Please use this link to access the list:

http://www.rosenlinks.com/411/Cyber

FOR FURTHER READING

Bazelon, Emily. *Sticks and Stones: Defeating the Culture of Bullying and Rediscovering the Power of Character and Empathy.* New York, NY: Random House, 2013.

Bily, Cynthia A. *The Internet.* Farmington Hills, MI: Greenhaven Press, 2012.

Brown, Tracy. *Cyberbullying: Online Safety.* New York, NY: Rosen Classroom, 2013.

Donovan, Sandra. *Communication Smarts: How to Express Yourself Best in Conversations, Texts, E-Mails, and More.* Minneapolis, MN: Twenty-First Century Books, 2013.

Harasymiw, Therese. *Cyberbullying and the Law.* New York, NY: Rosen Central, 2013.

Head, Honor. *How to Handle Cyberbullying.* Mankato, MN: Smart Apple Media, 2014.

Hinduja, Sameer, and Justin W. Patchin. *Bullying Beyond the Schoolyard: Preventing and Responding to Cyberbullying.* Thousand Oaks, CA: Corwin Press, 2009.

Ivester, Matt. *Lol—Omg! What Every Student Needs to Know About Online Reputation Management, Digital Citizenship, and Cyberbullying.* Reno, NV: Serra Knight, 2011.

Jacobs, Thomas A. *Teen Cyberbullying Investigated: Where Do Your Rights End and Consequences Begin?* Minneapolis, MN: Free Spirit, 2010.

Lohmann, Raychelle Cassada, and Julia V. Taylor. *The Bullying Workbook for Teens: Activities to Help You Deal with Social Aggression and Cyberbullying.* Oakland, CA: Instant Help Books, 2013.

Meyer, Stephenie, John Meyer, Emily Sperber, and Heather Alexander. *Bullying Under Attack: True Stories Written by Teen Victims, Bullies & Bystanders.* Deerfield Beach, FL: Health Communications, Incorporated, 2013.

Naik, Anita. *The Quick Expert's Guide to Safe Social Networking.* London, England: Wayland, 2014.

Parks, Peggy J. *Cyberbullying.* San Diego, CA: ReferencePoint Press, 2013.

Patchin, Justin W., and Sameer Hinduja. *Words Wound: Delete Cyberbullying and Make Kindness Go Viral.* Minneapolis, MN: Free Spirit, 2013.

Purcell, Mark C., and Jason R. Murphy. *Mindfulness for Teen Anger: A Workbook to Overcome Anger and Aggression Using MBSR and DBT Skills.* Oakland, CA: New Harbinger Publications, 2014.

Rogers, Vanessa. *Cyberbullying Activities to Help Children and Teens to Stay Safe in a Texting, Twittering, Social Networking World.* London, England: Jessica Kingsley, 2010.

Roleff, Tamara L. *Cyberbullying.* Detroit, MI: Greenhaven Press, 2012.

Ryan, Peter. *Online Bullying* (Teen Mental Health). New York, NY: Rosen Young Adult, 2011.

Savage, Dan. *It Gets Better: Coming Out, Overcoming Bullying, and Creating a Life Worth Living*. New York, NY: Dutton, 2011.

Sprague, Susan. *Coping with Cliques*. Oakland, CA: New Harbinger Publications, 2008.

Stuckey, Rachel. *Cyber Bullying*. New York, NY: Crabtree, 2013.

Subramanian, Mathangi. *Bullying: The Ultimate Teen Guide*. Lanham, MD: Rowman & Littlefield, 2014.

Withers, Jennie, and Phyllis Hendrickson. *Hey, Back Off! Tips for Stopping Teen Harassment*. Far Hills, NJ: New Horizon, 2011.

BIBLIOGRAPHY

CASAColumbia. "2011 National Teen Survey Finds: Teens Regularly Using Social Networking Sites Likelier to Smoke, Drink, Use Drugs." August 24, 2011. Retrieved September 20, 2014 (http://www.casacolumbia.org/newsroom/press-releases/2011-national-teen-survey-finds).

Centers for Disease Control and Prevention. "Suicide Prevention." January 9, 2014. Retrieved September 20, 2014 (http://www.cdc.gov/violenceprevention/pub/youth_suicide.html).

Eckerd, Marcia. "Cyberbullying: Parents Beware." Smart Kids with Learning Disabilities. Retrieved September 19, 2014 (http://www.smartkidswithld.org/?s=Cyberbullying%3A+Parents+Beware).

Elgot, Jessica. "Why Do Some Teens Troll Themselves Online?" *Huffington Post* UK, May 10, 2014. Retrieved September 20, 2014 (http://www.huffingtonpost.co.uk/2014/05/08/cyber-self-harm_n_5288148.html).

Gay, Lesbian & Straight Education Network. *Out Online: The Experiences of LGBT Youth on the Internet.* Retrieved September 19, 2014 (http://glsen.org/sites/default/files/out%20online%20FINAL.pdf).

Hemmen, Lucy. "Stressed Out Teen Girls: Cutting to Cope." *Psychology Today.* November 28, 2012. Retrieved September 20, 2014 (http://www

.psychologytoday.com/blog/teen-girls-crash
-course/201211/stressed-out-teen-girls-cutting
-cope).

Magid, Larry. "Researchers Dispel Myths About
Cyberbullying." *Huffington Post*, November
20, 2012. Retrieved September 19, 2014
(http://www.huffingtonpost.com/larry-magid/
cyberbullying_b_2162759.html).

National Center for Education Statistics. Table
230.40, in *Digest of Education Statistics*.
Retrieved September 19, 2014 (http://nces.ed.gov/
programs/digest/d13/tables/dt13_230.40.asp).

National Conference of State Legislatures. "State
Cyberstalking and Cyberharassment Laws."
December 5, 2013. Retrieved September 20, 2014
(http://www.ncsl.org/research/telecommunications
-and-information-technology/cyberstalking-and
-cyberharassment-laws.aspx).

NIH News. "Depression High Among Youth Victims
of School Cyber Bullying, NIH Researchers
Report. September 21, 2010 News Release—
National Institutes of Health (NIH)." Retrieved
September 20, 2014 (http://www.nih.gov/news/
health/sep2010/cichd-21.htm).

Nobullying.com: The Movement Against Bullying.
"Cyber Bullying Statistics 2014." Retrieved
September 19, 2014 (http://nobullying.com/
cyber-bullying-statistics-2014).

PACER's National Bullying Prevention Center.
"Bullying Statistics." Retrieved September 19,

2014 (http://www.pacer.org/bullying/about/
media-kit/stats.asp).

Parker, Ian. "The Story of a Suicide." *New Yorker*,
February 6, 2012. Retrieved September
19, 2014 (http://www.newyorker.com/
magazine/2012/02/06/the-story-of-a-suicide).

Patchin, Justin W., and Sameer Hinduja.
"Cyberbullying Facts." Cyberbullying Research
Center. Retrieved September 19, 2014 (http://
cyberbullying.us/facts).

Patchin, Justin W., and Sameer Hinduja. "Research."
Cyberbullying Research Center. Retrieved
September 19, 2014 (http://www.cyberbullying
.us/research.php).

Pokin, Steve. "Megan's Story." Megan Meier
Foundation. Retrieved September 19, 2014
(http://www.meganmeierfoundation.org/megans
-story.html).

Rosenbloom, Stephanie. "Dealing with Digital
Cruelty." *New York Times*, August 23, 2014.
Retrieved September 20, 2014 (http://www
.nytimes.com/2014/08/24/sunday-review/dealing
-with-digital-cruelty.html).

Sleglova, Veronika, and Alena Cerna. "Cyberbullying
in Adolescent Victims: Perception and Coping."
*Cyberpsychology: Journal of Psychosocial
Research on Cyberspace*, January 1, 2011.
Retrieved September 20, 2014 (http://www
.cyberpsychology.eu/view.php?cisloclanku
=2011121901).

Steffgen, Georges, Andreas König, Jan Pfetsch, and André Melzer. "Are Cyberbullies Less Empathic? Adolescents' Cyberbullying Behavior and Empathic Responsiveness." *Cyberpsychology, Behavior, and Social Networking* 14, no. 11 (2011): 643–48.

Stopbullying.com. "Federal Laws." Retrieved September 20, 2014 (http://www.stopbullying .gov/laws/federal/index.html).

Ybarra, Michelle. "The Top 5 Myths of Cyberbullying." *Psychology Today*, March 3, 2014. Retrieved September 19, 2014 (http://www .psychologytoday.com/blog/connected/201403/ the-top-5-myths-cyberbullying).

INDEX

disabilities, learning and social, 12
discrimination, 56, 58, 63
drugs and alcohol, 34, 36, 41, 51

E

eating disorders, 41, 46, 50, 55
Eckerd, Marcia, 9, 12
e-mail, 4, 30, 40, 54, 83
empathy, lack of, 16

F

Facebook, 11, 18–19, 37, 44, 74, 81, 83
face-to-face time with friends, 74–79
false identities, creating, 20–22, 26

G

gaming community, 25, 74, 82
Gay, Lesbian & Straight Education Network (GLSEN), 12

H

hacking, 23, 26, 27–29, 83
harassment, 56, 58
healing and moving on, 70–74

Hinduja, Sameer, 4, 8, 20, 45, 54
hurtful remarks, sending, 8–14

I

"I Choose" campaign, 93
information
  giving private, 23–26, 82–83
  stolen, 27–29
Instagram, 11
instant messaging, 4
isolation, 4, 18, 43, 50, 51, 73, 89

K

kindness, spreading, 89–94

L

labeling people, the problem with, 88
laws, cyberbullying, 56, 58–60
LGBT individuals, 12, 31
lies and rumors, spreading, 6, 14–19, 55, 85
lifestyle choices, 12–14

M

manipulation, 26, 37, 39
Meier, Megan, 22, 55

About the Author

Caitie McAneney is a writer and editor from Buffalo, New York. She studied creative writing, English, and psychology at Canisius College. She is the author of many children's nonfiction books, including several guidance books. As an author for children and young adults, she takes special interest in the psychological and interpersonal lives of young people.

Photo Credits